The Dr
FastForwardFramework

*Ten Steps To Help You
Live A Life You Love*

RB
Rossendale Books

Published by Lulu Enterprises Inc.
3101 Hillsborough Street
Suite 210
Raleigh, NC 27607-5436
United States of America

Published in paperback 2014
Category: Self Improvement
Copyright Dr Jane Cox © 2014
ISBN : 978-1-291-74243-5

About the author

Dr Jane Cox is an international human behavioural specialist and peak performance expert, specialising in life transformation.

She has changed the lives of thousands of people around the world, as well as helping hundreds of businesses of all types to achieve new levels of success.

Jane has worked with clients across the globe, and with well-known "gurus" such as Greg Secker, Andy Harrington, and Scott Harris.

Her suite of development programmes are always in high demand, and often with a waiting list – check out the details at www.newlevels.co.uk

Read what Jane's clients and delegates have to say about her:

"I've never met anyone who has been able to give me back my belief in myself, and then help me harness my talent, and help me move forward like Jane – amazing"　　　　Lisa D

"She gave me back my mojo! I'm now I'm a new man, or maybe just the one I was always meant to be!"　　　　Mike M

"She refused to give up on me even when I'd given up on me. Thank you for believing in me and holding my hand when the going got tough. Now I know I can do anything I choose to do because I've found my strength"　　　　Alex R

Contents

Introduction

"You only need to achieve the "impossible" once, for all things to become possible."

Dr Jane Cox

In today's fast-paced world we're all so busy dealing with our lives that we don't have the time or energy to sit down and think properly about where we're heading.

Some people feel mired in meaningless work, while others feel that they are making good forward progress, but they're not really sure if that progress is in a direction that they ultimately want. Still others feel overwhelmed and exhausted just thinking about doing anything so big and daunting as achieving goals that seem more of a hopeful dream than anything real and tangible.

How do we snap out of this mindset, and actually set goals that are real and meaningful for ourselves? How big or small do we make these goals? How do we decide what they are, and, especially if they're in an area that is completely different from our normal lives, how on earth do we even start to make progress towards those goals?

These 10 steps will take you through some of the fundamental and concrete strides that we can take towards achieving excellence in different areas of our lives. Whatever is most important to you, is where you need to focus your energy. Perhaps your career is a bit mundane for your liking? Perhaps a relationship needs to regain its spark, or perhaps a new relationship IS your goal.

Maybe you have always wanted to learn something that interests you greatly. Possibly health or fitness is where you want to be paying attention. Or maybe it's family or friends that need more love and attention, and a happy family life is top of your priority list. And usually, money is a driving goal for people. Whether you want enough to live comfortably and worry-free, or whether you want millions of spare pounds in your account, in this day and age, we can't ignore the impact, both positive and negative, money can have on our lives.

This set of 10 steps is pulled from our popular and successful "180/180" life turnaround programme, and I hope it gives you focus and a framework for thinking really carefully about what you want and how to make it happen, step by step.

Step number one is always the place to start, no matter what area of your life you want to work on!

Step I

Know where you`re coming from

"Understanding can overcome any situation, no matter how mysterious or insurmountable it may appear to be."
Norman Vincent Peale

First things first:

Where are you right now in your life? Not "where would you like to be", or "where were you a year ago", but where are you right now! The secret here is to be completely honest with yourself. Take the time to write down exactly where you are today in the following areas of your life:

a) your career

Just for clarification, your career encompasses any work related activities, so if you have more than one form of work, put them all in. Remember, they don't have to generate an income to qualify for this category, so if you do volunteer or charity work, that counts too.

b) your finances

Likewise with finances; If you have more than one form of income, make sure you include them all. Remember there are two sides to this point, your finances coming in, and your finances going out. Both aspects need to be under your control, rather than your life being under their control!

c) your love life

If you're in a relationship, how happy are you with that relationship? This includes your intimate relationship, the supportiveness you offer each other, your satisfaction with how you deal with mutual concerns, like raising your family, managing your money, shared activities, or compatibility with your levels of allowing each other to pursue your own interests.

If you don't have a love life, that's equally important. Is your absence of love life by choice or by circumstance? Would you like to build up a meaningful love interest with someone? Do you have someone already in mind, and you can't find the courage to move a potential relationship forward? Do you battle to meet new people? Do you have an idea of the type of person you ideally want to have as a partner?

d) your relationships with important family members

Whether you come from a big family, or a small family; Whether you're a close-knit bunch, or pursuing independent lives; Whether you're dealing with older relatives, younger relatives, same generation or different generation relationships, how happy are you with your family dynamic?

Are there relationships that need work, perhaps between parent and child, or step-family relationships? Are you happy with your relationships with the family members that are important to you?

e) your relationships with friends

Do you have a few really close friends, or a wide social circle? Do you fit in and enjoy the company of your circle of friends? Are there members of your group of friends that are particularly supportive to you? Alternatively, do you feel a bit lonely? Would you like to make a couple of close friendships, or do you crave to be part of a social circle? Do you find some of your friendships hard work?

f) your health and fitness

Think about your current levels of general health. Do you eat well? Are your energy levels high, or do you feel sluggish? Do you sleep well? Do you feel comfortable with your weight? Are there any recurring or chronic health conditions you may be dealing with? Are you fit enough to be able to play with your kids, or take a good walk, or keep your body supple and strong?

This is not about being a model, or an Olympic athlete. This is about your levels of happiness with your most important possession, your body. We can change our cars regularly, move homes, and change countries, but we have our same body for life. Do you feel happy about walking into your future in your body, and do you feel confident it has the strength, health and fitness to carry you through your life, no matter how long that life turns out to be?

g) your fun and recreation time

This is normally the first part of your life that gets culled when finances are tight, and yet it is an area of your life that is so important to maintaining your balance and giving you a break from some of the stresses that can wear us down.

Do you have hobbies that you can enjoy? Do you make time and effort to spend time with, and have fun with, your families or friends? Do you take holidays that give you an opportunity to rest and regenerate? Do you have variety and interest in your life? Do you allow yourself to have regular things in your diary that you can really look forward to enjoying?

h) your current personal learning and growth

This can be for career purposes, or just for self interest. The minute you stop learning or reading, and stop enjoying the discovery of new information, the quicker you'll find your career stalling, and your interest levels in many different areas dwindling.

It doesn't matter if it's formal education, or new experiences, sheer curiosity or the drive to learn something new, keeping your brain active and challenging yourself to try new things is what helps keep us engaged in our lives, and in our world. So whether it's learning a language, taking a course, trawling the Internet for information, or learning to paint or dance, are you keeping your brain stimulated and your areas of knowledge current?

i) your spiritual development

Just for the record, this does not necessarily have anything to do with religion! Whether you are religious or not, and if you are, which religion you follow, is not important. What is important is that you are happy with your place in the world, and that your life has purpose.

Spiritual development for many is keeping a healthy curiosity and an open mind. It is about feeling that your life has value and that you can make a difference, or leave a legacy. It is for most people the hope that, when you are dead and gone, something positive remains in the world, and you were responsible for creating it.

j) your personal space – home, office, car, etc

Think about the spaces that you occupy – mainly your home, your car, and your office. Are you happy with each of those areas of your life? Do you live in a home that you enjoy returning to at the end of a busy day? Is it tidy and does it make you feel comfortable? Do you like the area you live in? The condition of your home? Does it need tidying, or painting? Do you have a beautiful garden, or a lovely view? Does your house feel like a home?

Likewise, is your car reliable, comfortable, clean, tidy? Do you need to give it a service? Or take more care of it? Is your office space neat and tidy? Does it encourage you to be creative and productive? Is it a space in which you can comfortably pursue career growth, and get things done quickly and efficiently?

Keep an open mind and take the time to go through each of these ten sections properly. You'll often find that knowing where things can be improved, and making relatively small changes can really make a positive impact on your life.

STARTING POINT EXERCISE:

a/ career:

10

at a threshold of change
But all good

b/ finances:

5

marginally ready for
Retirement at a manner
to with I'm accepting

c/ love:

nothing

d/ relationships - family:

Good family relations

e/ relationships – friends:

good friend relations

f/ health and fitness: Health ok

Not as good physical fitness

g/ fun and recreation: Not as much as I would like - Love golf & travel

h/ personal learning and growth: Not as much as I would like i/ spiritual development:

not as much
I would like

j/ personal space:

_OK_

Some of these areas may be more important to you than other areas, and that's fine. But even in areas that are further down your list of importance, take the time to have a good look at them anyway. Perhaps part of the reason for any current frustrations or feelings of emptiness may be because your life may not be particularly well balanced, and probably having a good think about where you are in each area will give you a clearer idea of where you need to focus your attention.

Some of these areas will be in a much better state than others, and that may be because those are the areas that are most important to you. Alternatively it may be because some sort of calamity has befallen you in some part of your life, or that some other reason has caused an area of your life to be ignored. Possibly one or two of the areas may be really important to you, but it seems so overwhelming just trying to work out where to start that they've been left in a state of limbo. And of course there may be some areas that are just downright neglected.

Now that you've written down your starting points in all the different areas, go back through them, and give each area a score out of 10, rating how happy you currently are with that area, with 10 being the highest score, and 0 the lowest score. Now look at the following chart, and draw a line across each column based on your score for each of the areas.

Colour in the columns up to your rating line, and look at your result. This is the "BALANCE METER" of your life today, and of course the higher and more equal the levels are, the more likely you are to be feeling really happy about your life and excited about where it is taking you. Sometimes we need to see things in black and white to realise just how much of the whole is coloured in, and just how much balance, or lack of balance we have in our life.

LIFE BALANCE METER

	A	B	C	D	E	F	G	H	I	J
1	ꙮ									
2										
3										
4										
5		X								
6										
7										
8										
9										
10			X							

Take a look at the lines you've drawn on the tops of your columns. Are they more or less equal, indicating a relatively balanced and rounded starting point? Are they hugely staggered, indicating that some areas are paying the price for progress you've achieved on other areas?

Without intentionally setting out to destroy anything, what we sometimes do is sacrifice one area of our life while we work on another, assuming that when we're ready, it'll all come together, and we can just step back into the neglected area without a worry. Unfortunately though, this is often not the case. We all know of broken relationships caused by excessive workloads, or health sacrificed on the altar of nights out with mates, or finances straining under the weight of excessive fun and recreation!

Ideally, the straighter the line across the top of your chart, and of course the higher up each column it runs, the more balanced and rounded your life is, and the less likely you are to suffer from frustrations and irritations, and the more likely you are to be experiencing that contentment and happiness that a good life brings!

Now that we've found our starting points, we're better equipped to move on to step number two...

Step 2

Understand what you want and why you want it

"Though no one can go back and make a new start, anyone can start from now and make a brand new ending.".

Carl Bard

What do you want, and why do you want it?

This sounds a bit odd, but let me explain myself! Sometimes it's so long between setting a goal and getting around to achieving it, that we may not even be that motivated by that goal now – it may no longer be something that's relevant to you.

Often, we know we want change and positive forward momentum, but we can't quite put our finger on what that change or what that movement needs to be.

Another common problem that I find amongst delegates on my 180/180 Programme, is that they feel unmotivated to achieve their goals and can't understand why this is the case. Often on closer analysis, it becomes clear that the goal in question is not actually an authentic goal.

Unauthentic goals can come from a number of different places: Did one of your parents want you to achieve a goal that they perhaps hadn't achieved themselves? This is a common issue, where we have heard something for so long that we assume it is a goal that belongs to us, while instead it really belongs to someone else and has been foisted on to us.

It is not your responsibility to live out your parents' goals, or your teacher's goals for you. It is your responsibility to achieve all the incredible things that your life, your skills, your talents and your dreams were designed to fulfill, and I can pretty much guarantee that your parents will be thrilled to have produced a successful and happy adult!

Often, we have been sucked into believing that we want to achieve a goal, just because it's a goal that lots of other people seem to think is important, and so we feel that it must be important and it should be on our list of goals too.

Perhaps your friends embarked on a group fitness campaign, and even though you are happy with your levels of fitness and the times of their gym visits mess up your free time and feels like a bit of a drag, you ended up being persuaded to join in. So now you have the interesting dilemma of feeling fed up about putting in the work to achieve your "goal", and you may actually start to feel that "working towards your goals" is an overrated thing to do! Of course it's not, but working towards someone else's goals could well be a drag! So if you've ever felt this way, perhaps now it's beginning to make sense to you!

Go back through the ten different areas in Step One, and decide what YOU want in those different areas. If something doesn't "feel" right to you, it probably isn't actually a goal that is really important to you anymore. **Throw those ones out**, and replace them with things that you KNOW would make a huge positive difference in your life.

Completing this exercise will give us a good starting point to work from, and we can start putting together your steps of progress! (Which will lead us nicely on to step three …)

GOAL RE-ASSESSMENT EXERCISE:

a) career:

_____

_____

_____

_____

_____

_____

_____

b) finances:

_____

_____

_____

_____

_____

_____

_____

c) love:

_____

_____

_____

_____

_____

_____

_____

d) relationships - family:

_____

_____

_____

_____

_____

_____

_____

e) relationships – friends:

_____

_____

_____

_____

_____

_____

_____

f) health and fitness:

_____

_____

_____

_____

_____

_____

_____

g) fun and recreation:

_____

_____

_____

_____

_____

_____

_____

h) personal learning and growth:

_____

_____

_____

_____

_____

_____

_____

i) spiritual development:

_____

_____

_____

_____

_____

_____

_____

j) personal space:

_____

_____

_____

_____

_____

_____

_____

Step 3

Put a time and destination stamp on your goals

*"Discipline is the bridge between goals and
accomplishment."*
Jim Rohn

Remember that wise old adage: A goal is only a goal when it has a time by which it needs to be achieved, and a good solid substance to it. Without that, it's just a woolly thought that is highly unlikely to ever become something real.

Your job now is to go through your goals, and prioritise them: Which goals would make the biggest positive impact on your life? Which ones are more urgent than the others? Which ones really excite you at the prospect of achieving that goal? This will help us when it comes time to put dates onto the achievement of each goal.

Go through each of your goals and flesh them out. If you want to lose weight and improve your health, how would you like that to impact your life? Rather than just a "keep fit and eat less" wishy-washy idea, give it parameters. For example, "I will lose 8 kilograms and have the strength and stamina to complete a 5km fun run by 20th March", or "I will fit into my size 10 dresses with ease, and be able to beat my best friend on a squash court by my birthday this year."

The more real and tangible we can make our goals, the more easily our brain is able to accept that it can easily become part of your reality. A lot of self-help books will tell you to focus on your goal, and try to imagine it, smell it, feel it, taste it, etc. Why do they do this? So that your body can fully embrace that goal. However I've watched people try to do this. They'll often close their eyes for a few minutes, scrunch up their faces, and "concentrate" on each of these senses in relation to that goal, and then open their eyes and consider their job done.

This of course has limited success! Rather than concentrating on the senses, perhaps it would be better to create a "daydream" of you having achieved that goal. Perhaps focusing on how you FEEL, dressed in your size 10 tennis outfit, feeling amazing because you've finally won a game, and you feel fit enough and on such a high, that you feel you could comfortably start another game!

Imagine wiping the well earned sweat off your brow, and picking up your water bottle, savouring that cold refreshing water, and drinking in the feelings of success!

Perhaps your goal is learning a new language. Let's choose Italian for the purpose of this example. And your reward for doing so will be to take yourself on a wonderful holiday to Italy. Imagine soaking in the scenery, and perhaps sitting in a lovely pavement café eating fabulous fresh Italian food, followed by a delicious cup of coffee that tastes just the way that coffee smells, and being able to follow all the Italian conversations the locals are having around you.

You feel comfortable ordering in Italian, and can even perhaps share a joke with the waiter, or have a casual chat with the Italian sitting at the next table about the glorious weather. FEEL that success, and that knowledge that you have gained a skill that you will be able to use always, and which will come with you into your future. Imagine stretching back in your chair after that good meal, feeling the sunshine on your face, and the energy around you and knowing that you have truly earned the right to enjoy and savour your fabulous trip.

The more "real" you can make your goals, and the better you can imagine the reality of living in that new part of your life that the achievement of that goal will open, the more your mind accepts it as reality and starts recognising opportunities and steps that can be taken by you towards turning that goal into your reality.

The benefit of creating what almost seems like a daydream sequence, is that whenever you are feeling stressed or overwhelmed by the next step you need to take, or the fulfillment of a particular part of that goal path, you can give yourself a few minutes to breathe deep, relax into your daydream, and inspire yourself to get cracking and get through the scary or boring piece of the journey that is sitting right in front of you!

Also, by putting a time limit on your goals, you do two things: you put yourself under a positive form of pressure, and you also have an exit point that you can focus on.

The fact is that no matter how badly you want a goal, there will be some more boring and less exciting parts to some of the steps towards even the best goal on the planet, and most of us can put up with stuff we don't like, or something that seems hard, if we know it won't last forever. If you know that step in your goal will be done and dusted by the end of the month, doesn't that make it easier to buckle down and get it done?

Lastly, with this step is important to remember that some of your goals might fit in with your current work or life situation, and can fit in quite comfortably alongside your normal daily routine, but some of them might be towards setting up a whole new career, or doing something like learning a language that needs to be slotted in around your existing schedule.

Keep this is mind when you're working out the time limits you're setting yourself. You can't be neglecting the work that brings in the bread and butter while you work on something that'll make you rich in five years time! With your timings, you need to be realistic to your current life circumstances, but tight enough to push yourself outside of your comfort zone and inject a level of pressure and urgency upon you!

Most of the worthwhile achievements we make in our lives are achieved under the most challenging of circumstances, but that determination pays off in spades. The more challenging the circumstances, usually the more rewarding the goal and the more appreciative we are of our own abilities to rise to great heights and overcome challenges and obstacles!

Write down your top goals in the following exercise sheet, trying if you can to prioritise them in the order in which you would ideally like to achieve them. This then will lead us on to our very important fourth step:

1.
Goal:_____

_____

Details:_____

_____

_____

_____

_____

_____

Completion
Date:_____

2.
Goal:_____

_____

Details:_____

_____

_____

_____

_____

Completion
Date:_____

3.
Goal:_____

_____

Details:_____

_____

_____

_____

_____

_____

Completion
Date:_____

4.
Goal:_____

_____

Details:_____

_____

_____

_____

_____

_____

Completion
Date:_____

5.

Goal:_____

_____

Details:_____

_____

_____

_____

_____

_____

Completion
Date:_____

6.

Goal:_____

_____

Details:_____

_____

_____

_____

_____

_____

Completion
Date:_____

7.
Goal:_____

_____

Details:_____

_____

_____

_____

_____

_____

Completion
Date:_____

8.
Goal:_____

_____

Details:_____

_____

_____

_____

_____

Completion
Date:_____

9.

Goal:_____

_____

Details:_____

_____

_____

_____

_____

_____

Completion
Date:_____

10.

Goal:_____

_____

Details:_____

_____

_____

_____

_____

Completion
Date:_____

Step 4

Focus on just two or three goals at a time

"I don't care how much power, brilliance or energy you have, if you don't harness it and focus on a specific target, and hold it there, you're never going to achieve as much as your ability warrants."   Zig Ziglar

Look at the goals you have in each of the ten sections in step one. Now choose just two or three of those goals for immediate attention. Preferably, choose a mix of relatively short term and longer term goals. Or perhaps a couple of goals that seem like they would be easier to achieve, and another that would take a bit more time and effort.

You are not rejecting any of the other goals, or belittling them in any way, but one of the biggest challenges I see with some of my delegates, especially those with very full lives, or who are very ambitious and driven, is that they want to achieve everything now! Well the problem is that, if you have ten really key goals to achieve, and you launch into trying to do them all at once, your attention becomes far too scattered, with each goal probably getting 10% of your drive and energy, and a very fractured form of focus! The result? None of them actually get finished!

Without a doubt, you would get all 10 goals achieved much quicker and better by working on a couple of them at a time, finishing those, and moving on to the next two or three goals! Try it, and you can let me know how it goes!

There are four tricks to this goal selection:

a) Look for the goals that would make the biggest impact on your life the quickest. We are motivated by experiencing positive change, so let's give ourselves the very thing we look for! If you will look like a million dollars when you shed 5kg in time for your Birthday dinner in two months, and you know just the outfit you could wear beautifully if you shed that weight, then do it!

Two months is not a long time to achieve a goal that will have such an immediate positive impact on how you perceive yourself. And aiming to lose between ½ and 1 kg a week through sensible diet and exercise is perfectly realistic!

In fact, if you really believe in your goal strongly enough, go and buy that outfit that you would wear, and every week put it on to encourage yourself with how much easier the zip is to pull up, or how much flatter your stomach looks.

Perhaps finishing off that qualification that you need for work would put you in line for a good promotion or increase by the end of the year, and you just haven't got around to finishing it. That's another one that might be able to be achieved successfully in a matter of months, and the promotion and the increase in income would make a huge impact on your life. Choose that one too. The dramatic differences these goals will make to your life will fire you up to move on to the next one, and keep your enthusiasm and energy high!

b) Some goals work well being achieved together. Lets look at the goals we've set ourselves in this example. There is no reason why tackling a few kilograms and gaining a qualification would not be easily achievable together. Now let's add in a third goal. Let's say you want to spring clean your house from top to bottom. Go through all your cupboards, chuck out all the stuff you've accumulated that you no longer need, reorganise your bookshelves, and deep clean all the carpets.

Well how great would you feel if you've lost that weight, increased your income and de-cluttered and tidied your home? Wouldn't it make you feel fantastic? Wouldn't you feel strong, and confident, and capable? Imagine how well positioned you'd be mentally, emotionally and physically to work towards your next two or three goals, like maybe saving for a once in a lifetime holiday to your dream destination, and learning to cook amazing Thai food? Or maybe moving on to another qualification, or going to art lessons, or learning to master a musical instrument that you've always fancied being able to pick up and play?

c) Some goals will be more fun to achieve than others, so when you're putting together your two or three goals maximum at any time, make sure that you don't just do the fun ones and leave the less appealing work ones, knowing you're highly unlikely to ever get around to doing them!

If you have an easier and a more difficult goal, or a shorter term or a longer term goal to work on at the same time, your progress in one will often spur you on to make progress in the other. So in our example above, perhaps losing weight is a challenge for you, because perhaps you're a boredom eater. The beauty of the above combination, is that when you feel yourself wanting to habitually reach for the biscuit tin or the chocolate bar, instead, tidy out a shelf in your cupboard and distract yourself with an activity that will help achieve one goal – that of spring-cleaning – while also conveniently helping you to achieve the second goal of weight loss!

d) And lastly, make sure that your goals that you are running at the same time come from completely different parts of your goal sheet. That way, boredom and lethargy is far less likely to creep in. If all your goals were work related, your work-life balance would go out of kilter very quickly, but if you had a personal goal, like sorting out your house, as well as a work related goal of completing your qualification, then when you got a bit fed up with working towards one of them, you could switch your attention to something completely different. And if both of them starting getting to you, you could go on a long walk, which will help with your health related goal too!

YOUR INITIAL GOALS:

1.
Goal:_____
_____

Details:_____
_____
_____
_____
_____
_____

Completion
Date:_____

2.
Goal:_____
_____

Details:_____
_____
_____
_____
_____
_____

Completion
Date:_____

3.
Goal:_____

_____

Details:_____

_____
_____
_____
_____
_____

Completion
Date:_____

Now there is another little mistake we tend to make, so before you settle with finality on which goals to do first, or which goals are most important to you, be sure to look carefully at step number five.

Step 5

Work on your strengths, not your weaknesses

"Success is achieved by developing our strengths, not eliminating our weaknesses."
Marilyn vos Savant

But surely this is contrary to everything we're taught? Surely, it's our weaknesses we need to work on, so that we can have greater strength in all areas? If we're already strong at something, surely that's a reason to push it further down our goal priority list?

This is such a common misperception, and I find that its correction is one of the things that gives my delegates the biggest grin on their faces and bounce in their steps. None of us need to be all things to all people – that's not how we're built as human beings! In this day and age there are such a huge amount of areas that we feel we need to at least have a working knowledge of, that we find ourselves floundering around, feeling flustered and frustrated by our lack of "knowledge" or "ability" in areas we are made to feel are key to our success.

What happens then? Well, we end up putting a lot of time and effort into trying to master things that we're not particularly good at, and that are of very little real interest to us. We lose faith in ourselves and in our abilities. We hold ourselves responsible for our lack of success in certain areas, and that completely undermines our self-confidence that we're good at anything at all! We're our own worst enemies, concentrating on our supposed shortcomings, rather than concentrating on our talents and interests.

It fascinates me when I'm getting feedback from delegates on my course about their achievements since our last session, and inevitably, especially at the beginning of our time together, they are so quick to beat themselves up!

They may have aimed at getting five pieces of work completed over the course of a week, and only managed to get four done. Instead of then feeling proud about four pieces of major forward process, I find the tendency is to beat themselves up for not managing to complete the fifth piece of work.

Wow, we're our own hardest taskmasters, which would be great if it encouraged us to work harder, but instead it tends to cause us to want to give up altogether!

We need to remember that there are plenty of people who have amazing abilities and a love for the very things that perhaps we can't do or don't enjoy doing. Use their talents and abilities, and take that pressure off yourself! That's why we've all got such different interests and talents, so that we can complement each other, and take unnecessary pressure off each other's shoulders.

Your time is far more valuably spent getting better and better at your particular talents or areas of expertise. When this happens you can charge so much more for what you do, which of course gives you more cash to spread around the other folk who are working on the other areas, and following their dreams too. In our 21st century work, we look for excellence in highly specialised fields. And I have yet to find somebody criticise a life-saving heart surgeon for his inability to cook, or a talented seamstress for not being good at writing!

I think we're all familiar with that old adage "Jack of all trades, Master of none". Is this what you've been trying to do? By focusing on your weaknesses, you're concentrating on what you can't do. How good is this for your self esteem? How positively are you going to focus on stuff you don't particularly enjoy doing, and which you just don't naturally do as well? The answer of course, is not very well! You're likely to feel very lethargic and unmotivated about it. And this is your body giving you a fundamental clue – you shouldn't be investing that energy into it! Do what you love, follow your passion, and success will surely follow!

If we spend our time working on our weaknesses, and neglecting to work on our strengths, what we're really working towards is mediocrity in all things. If we work on making our strengths even more spectacular, we're working on excellence. One day when you're gone, would you rather leave a legacy of Mediocrity, or a legacy of Excellence? I know for sure the legacy I'm aiming to leave!!

Now go back through your goals carefully, Which ones of them are pursuing your excellence, and which ones are covering areas that you can sensibly walk away from? For those which may be in hot pursuit of your weaknesses, look at the areas in which you've set those goals. Is there perhaps another goal that you can set yourself that pursues your passion in that area?

Just one final word on this: There are always some things that we should be doing that we don't particularly enjoy doing! If you live in a household, for example, where nobody enjoys cooking or cleaning, things would quickly deteriorate into chaos if one of you does not step forward and take charge. A lack of doing this would result in a deterioration of your physical environment, and probably your relationships with your family or flatmates!

This is not an escape clause for not doing what needs to be done. With examples like this one, you have three choices: You can have a goal to improve your environment because you enjoy the results of the work it would take, even if not the work itself. And work on it. Or, perhaps you can persuade the rest of the family to join you in each taking on one part of the household, or one main meal every week, and split the load, making it easier for you all, and building your respect and appreciation of each other. Or you can work hard enough, and make enough money, to be able to pay somebody else to clean and tidy your home, or cook your meals!

A positive way of tackling this is perhaps to have as part of your goal, finding ways to streamline your running of your home so that it can be done easily and effectively in just half an hour of disciplined work every day. Or doing your cooking efficiently, perhaps by cooking double quantities of each meal so you can freeze a full meal every day and halve the amount of cooking you need to do every month!

Neglect of important areas, no matter how you feel about them, is not an option!! However efficiency and time management is always an option, and is something we cover in great detail in our 180/180 Programme.

Right, so now you should have established where you are in all the different sectors of your life. You should have clear ideas of what you want to achieve in some or all of those areas, you should be clear that they are goals that are genuinely important to YOU and not pulled from your long distant past, or from an influential relative.

You should know which goals will, when completed, add the biggest noticeable difference to your life, and you should have your primary list of goals selected. Those two or three goals that you're going to focus your time, energy and attention on first. You should have a realistic time frame against each of these goals – Long enough for the goal to realistically be achievable, yet tight enough to keep you on track and not give you time to stray from your goal journey. I think this means that the next step must be pretty obvious!

Just to allow for a complete tweak and refinement of your three primary goals, here is another worksheet for you:

1.
Goal:_____

_____

Details:_____

_____

_____

_____

_____

Completion
Date:_____

2.
Goal:_____

_____

Details:_____

_____

_____

_____

_____

Completion
Date:_____

3.
Goal:_____

_____

Details:_____

_____

_____

_____

_____

_____

Completion
Date:_____

Step 6

Get started!

"What is not started today, is never finished tomorrow"
Johann Wolfgang von Goethe

Yup. There's no getting away from it. The surest way to achieve your goals is to start putting in the effort towards them! Up until this stage, they're not real. They're just woolly ideas that are moving nowhere.

I'm a great believer in positive thinking, and I do genuinely believe that by thinking positively, and using affirmations, and all those good things, that we can certainly prime our minds to be open to recognising opportunities that tie up beautifully will our aims and goals. But many of these books tread lightly on the next important part of the equation – **TAKE POSITIVE ACTION!!!!**

Your "daydream" needs to become your reality, and the fact is that you have the power to make it so. In fact, you have the power to create any reality you want, you just need to put in the determination, focus, time, effort and energy. And of course as you start achieving really good meaningful goals, you'll be more and more open to recognising your true worth and ability to create your destiny. But that is another subject dealt with in another part of the course. Our aim right now is to get momentum going.

What happens with many people is that, while they really want to achieve a goal, it seems like such a big and impossible task that they don't know where to start! But remember, the journey towards any goal is just that – a journey. So the first thing that we need to do is to create our journey plan.

The easiest way to do this is as follows: Get a clean sheet of paper, and draw a straight line, either left to right, or up and down the page. I'd be really interested to get feedback on which line appeals best to you to work with – I'm not going to tell you here which one works better for the most people, but what I have noticed is that line preference is often linked to left- or right- handedness. So please let me know which direction you use and which is your dominant hand. I'm very curious!

Anyway, at one end of the line, either the left hand side, or the bottom of the line, write down where you are right now in achieving that goal. If it's a weight loss goal, how much do you want to lose? If it's a qualification goal, where are you at the moment in the attainment of that qualification? If it's to run a marathon, what is your current running capability and distance? If it's a new skill or language, where do you sit now (often easiest to illustrate in percentage of where you are against your 100% total goal in that area), etc. I'm sure you've got the picture!

On the other end of the line, write your final goal. The holiday to celebrate the successful acquisition of a new language. The Size 10 dress and 5kg weight loss – whatever it is. And put your time and destination "stamp" on that end of your line.

Now think about the actual journey. When you're driving, for example, from London to Edinburgh, do you need to be able to see Edinburgh to reach it? No. Do you need to be able to know, right now at the start, the different twists and turns your road may take? No! Do you need to know what other drivers are half way along the route already? No. You just need to know where you're headed. Picture the beautiful Castle gazing down over its characterful city of Edinburgh. And get going!

There are a couple of things that you ideally do need to know to make your journey easier. You need to be able to see the next piece of road directly in front of your car, and it helps if you know where your first petrol and refreshment stop is, so you can plan the FIRST PART of your journey accordingly. That is all. However, if you're planning on making the journey a bit easier on yourself, it might also help to know the other three or four refreshment stops that would be most convenient for you to stop at along your journey.

So let's take this information, and apply it to our timeline. First, as far as you can, put in the obvious steps along the way towards your goal. Just like it is highly unlikely that your stops on your journey to Edinburgh with be exactly equidistant, it is unlikely the broad-brush steps towards your goal will be exactly the same size. But they could give you a good guideline of reasonable stations along your journey, which can become smaller goals in their own right.

For example, losing weight is an easy one. You could have 1kg stations 5 times along your timeline to lose 5kgs. Completing a qualification might be a bit more textured. Perhaps for this you need to buy three more text books. Complete two assignments each in three different subjects, do your final study or revision, and pass three separate exams.

In this case, the assignments may be relatively well spread, but the exams might be a day apart from each other, and it may take a week for the books you ordered off the Internet to be delivered. You might have a week's study leave from work, or maybe you need to do all your final revision in your own time. It really doesn't matter. Mark each of these obvious steps, in the right order, along your timeline.

Now, take the first piece of your line – your starting "now" point, to your first "rest stop" or sub goal. Draw this line the same length as your complete goal line.

On a separate piece of paper, write down as many different things as you can think of that you will need to do in order to achieve that ONE STEP of your goal journey line. Ideally, each step needs to be small enough to be able to be completed in one sitting, so depending on your time availability, each step should take anything from a matter of minutes, to a few hours.

When you've written down as many individual mini-steps as you can, put them into their order of progress. Don't worry if this is a bit fluid – there is no law stating that you HAVE to do things in a certain order. Just try and be more or less thoughtful about the sensible and likely order of getting things done.

Remember you are only doing this for the first step of the goal. If you start right now getting tied up in the nitty gritty of some part of the journey that is still a couple of months away, you're likely to not be in full possession of the facts of what needs to be achieved then. Just focus on NOW. Write each of these mini-steps along the second line. Now you're well prepared to get going!

Here are a couple of examples, to give you a clearer idea of how to do this:

WEIGHT LOSS INITIAL TIMELINE

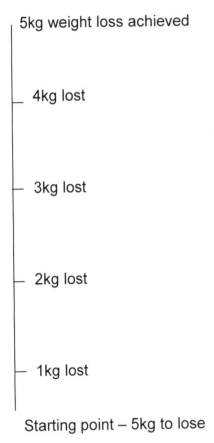

5kg weight loss achieved

4kg lost

3kg lost

2kg lost

1kg lost

Starting point – 5kg to lose

Now let's look at that intial weight loss timeline – **Kilogram number one is the only one we focus on**.

Perhaps the steps you feel you want to take towards this goal, assuming you want to reach that first goalpost in, say, one week, might be as follows:

A 30 minute brisk walk three times during the week. Two visits to the gym. Buying some good nutritious vegetables and preparing them, so that you can grab them out of the fridge and add them to your meal, perhaps in place of some of the carbohydrates you might ordinarily have with those meals. And avoiding that late-afternoon chocolate bar every day from Monday to Friday!

You also decide to cut back on your weekend alcohol intake. The "avoidance" goals, such as the chocolate and the alcohol, also need to be listed as separate goals in this case.

Your "mini-goals", In order, then would be as follows

Mon: Vegetable purchase, vegetable preparation, no chocolate,
Tues: High veg low starch main meal, brisk walk, no chocolate
Wed: High veg low starch main meal, gym visit, no chocolate
Thurs: High veg low starch main meal, brisk walk, no chocolate
Fri: High veg low starch main meal, gym visit, no chocolate
Sat: High veg low starch main meal, brisk walk, one small glass wine spritzer
Sun: High veg low starch main meal, no alcohol, weigh in, one chocolate bar.

Sun: 1/ High veg low starch main meal 2/ no alcohol
3/ one choc bar
1kg weight loss achieved – Day Seven

Sat: 1/ High veg low starch main meal 2/ brisk walk
3/ one small gls wine

Fri: 1/High veg low starch main meal 2/ gym visit
3/ no chocolate

Thurs: 1/ High veg low starch main meal 2/ brisk walk
3/ no chocolate

Wed: 1/ High veg low starch main meal 2/ gym visit
3/ no chocolate

Tues: 1/ High veg low starch main meal 2/ brisk walk
3/ no chocolate

Mon: 1/ Vegetable purchase 2/ vegetable preparation
3/ no chocolate,

Starting point – 1kg to lose in 7 days

How much easier and more motivating is that week's goals now? Every day, you're ticking off three separately achieved mini-goals. It puts the week into perspective. One sensibly portioned meal, one indulgence avoided, one piece of exercise completed, and your targets for the day have been met.

You can see that you do still have treats in the plan, but maybe one glass of wine is in place of your normal half bottle, and your weekly chocolate is one out of seven you would normally eat in a week. They give you something to look forward to, or reward yourself with. You don't need to find time to exercise and go grocery shopping on the same day. You don't need to feel guilty about not exercising on a couple of the days, because the week plan makes it clear you don't have to do that. And your chance of losing that kilogram is relatively high.

This is also now not too onerous a week to repeat another five or seven times until you've reached your 5kg weight loss goal. I've included a couple of examples of what this point is about. Hopefully it'll give you an idea of how best to tackle your timeline. Now, you don't need to worry about tomorrow's walk, you can just concentrate on one visit to the gym, for example.

The simple act of successfully climbing into bed each night having crossed off just three easily achievable steps keeps you focused on your success, rather than feeling like a failure. How easy does it now seem to be, to fit into that lovely dress in two months time?!

Of course, as you achieve each of the original bigger steps in your goal journey, do two things: Take time to acknowledge the work that you've done and the progress you've made, and reward yourself in a way that works for you. And then take the next of the bigger steps and go through the same process as well as you can, breaking that next step into its mini-goals, and so on, and so on, until you find yourself feeling on top of the world because that goal is done and dusted! That's when you need to reward yourself really well! And we'll talk about this a bit later…

Your turn….

Goal number one – Initial timeline:

Goal number one: Detailed timeline (of step one only)

Goal number two: Initial timeline

Goal number two: Detailed timeline (of step one only)

Goal number three: Initial timeline

Goal number three: Detailed timeline (of step one only)

Next, take the first one or two little items from each of your goal journey-lines, remembering each of them should be no longer than a couple of hours maximum, and DO THEM. The biggest challenge most people have is getting over that initial inertia, and once a project is started, and the momentum gathers, the journey gets easier and easier. As you complete the mini-tasks, run a highlighting pen through it. This way you can see real progress, and see those bright highlighting stripes moving up the line, or towards the right of that line, as you achieve more and more.

Don't look at the big goal other than as a reminder of how fabulous it'll be to achieve that goal. Don't worry about steps that are way in the future. That's like worrying about a mountain pass when you're driving through a valley, or worrying about a motorway onramp when you're meandering down a country road. Just do what you're doing right now. Any goal, no matter how big, is achieved by doing one thing at a time, and preferably doing it well.

However, even the best laid plans can go slightly awry, and this is why it's important to get your head around that little bugger in step seven:

Step 7

Understand and blitz procrastination

paralysis procrastination analysis stalling indecision decisions

"Procrastination is opportunity's assassin"
Victor Kiam

What is procrastination, and why do all of us, to different extents, fall prey to this particular challenge? Well, procrastination is simply losing the impetus to do the next step. And it often involves an incredible amount of energy being spent on doing other avoidance type tasks, or in feeling guilty, or in worrying about how we're ever going to achieve the bigger goal if we can't even manage to do a single step in a goal. And nobody is immune to this particular issue, it's just some people have managed the art of controlling it, and taking back charge of their own life.

We all know what procrastination feels like. And we all know how frustrated and fed up we feel when we have procrastinated and gotten behind in our task or goal. Why does it happen?

Well, there are a few reasons why we might fall prey to procrastination, so let's look at a few of those reasons, because often when we understand why something happens, we're far better equipped to know how to overcome it.

Firstly, perhaps you genuinely are so exhausted that even doing a 30min task just seems too much to handle. Have you been trying to fit far too much into a day? Are you sleeping badly? Is your lifestyle having a negative effect on your energy levels? Do you eat badly, or drink too much, or indulge in too much sugar, leading to sugar highs and sugar slumps?

If any of these things form part of your reality, we need to move the solving of these problems right up to the top of our goal list, because non-achievement of improving your diet/sleep patterns/time management/general health is having a really significant domino effect into your ability to achieve the rest of your goals.

Often people feel guilty for feeling tired, or don't want to admit that they live on fast food, or that they can't manage their time, and of course that in itself is counter-productive to your life balance. These are all areas that we cover in a fair amount of detail on our course, and we work with a number of effective time management tools, but it is essential for you to pinpoint your physical challenges, and find ways to deal with and rise above them.

Another problem with procrastination is that often the task at hand is so dull and boring that we just can't work up the enthusiasm to actually get it done. Once again, there are a couple of reasons why this might be the case, so let's look at how we can deal with them.

Firstly, maybe you're sitting on your couch, having just had a manic day at work, and you don't feel like trudging around your local park for your "brisk walk" challenge. Maybe you're looking at your assignment questions, and you just can't bear the thought of plowing your way through the paper. Maybe the cupboard door you've opened just reveals a chaos that looks impossible to tidy up.

The best solution to this is to change your focus. Take a different walk, perhaps down some local country lane. Challenge yourself to count how many dogs you see/types of flowers you spot/birds you can count/cars you pass, during that walk. This way, you're more focused on your own "game" rather than on the process of walking itself.

While you're walking, concentrate on what you can feel, see, or smell while you're walking – The soft breeze on your face, the scent of the flowers, or the buds coming up behind the blossomed flowers. Perhaps it's the sound of the leaves rustling, the hum of car engines, or the shouts of workmen on a building site. And enjoy the sheer variety and texture of what you are able to experience in one short 30 minute walk.

Feel how your body relaxes after a day cooped up in the office, or perhaps enjoy watching your dog revel in spending time with you outdoors.

For the assignment example, perhaps what you want to do is one of two things, both of which work really well when you're battling to get your head around getting something done. Firstly, you might want to break it down into even smaller steps. If there are 5 sections to the assignment, split it into 5 smaller steps instead of viewing it as one big job, so you can enjoy the feeling of making progress.

Then when you get to the end of the first section you're crossing an achievement off your list, rather than concentrating on the whole, still-to-be-completed task. When you finish the third section, you can allow yourself to feel proud of the fact that you've passed the half-way mark, and you're now on the homeward run.

Often we procrastinate simply because we haven't broken the task down into small enough sections. It often helps to look at the task you're avoiding and spend a couple of minutes breaking it down into smaller constituent parts.

You can use this to get through your walk as well – Break your total journey into landmarks. The house on the corner, the stream that runs across the road, the newsagent on the left, the top of the lane... It makes it so easy to achieve something when you allow yourself to just focus on the "right now" instead of getting bogged down with too much at a time.

Another way of tackling that "slumped on the couch and can't be bothered to move" lethargy, is to promise yourself that, if you complete that hour-long task, you will reward yourself by slumping on the couch and watching your favourite television programme, or read a couple of chapters of a book you're really enjoying.

What works very well for me personally, is challenging myself to achieve a certain amount of stuff in a set time span. I will, for example, choose a mini-goal that I reckon would realistically take an hour, and challenge myself to get it done in 45 minutes! I'll set myself an alarm. Or put my stop watch on a 45 minute countdown, and I will immerse myself in that task as completely as possible! I will do things as quickly and efficiently as I possibly can. And I won't let anything distract me from that task.

I still get a bit of a thrill when my alarm goes off, and the task is done in the shorter time span, essentially giving me back 15 minutes that I thought would belong to that task. I'll often use this time to reward myself for my blitz. Perhaps by sitting down with a lovely cup of tea, or phoning a friend, or having a warm shower, or whatever I think would be a really enjoyable use of those 15 minutes.

This "time blitz" approach can be done another way, which works just as effectively for me. For example, imagine my mini-goal is to tidy a shelf in my cupboard, and I've allocated an hour per shelf. (I know what you're thinking – I must have a hell of a lot of stuff on those shelves!). What I'll do is set my alarm or stop-watch for that hour, and see how much I can get done in that time.

Perhaps if I push myself and focus well, I can get two shelves sorted in that hour, or sort out all the cupboards in my kitchen, or write a full chapter of my book. Each time I do this, I try to better my results from the last hourly challenge. That way, I'm certain that my hour is well used, I know I can keep good focus for that limited time span, and I'm competing against my most successful opponent – myself!

You'll be amazed at just how efficient you can become when you learn the art of focus, and because you're focused on speed, you can spot all sorts of clever ways at trimming the excesses off your task, and identifying the things that don't really add value but just add time to the tasks you undertake. You become a mean, keen blitzing demon!

I run a whole workshop on the areas of time management and of procrastination, because if we can conquer those two challenges, we are automatically far better equipped to achieve any goal we wish really efficiently, and probably more quickly than many other people would be able to manage, but hopefully these two steps will give you some sensible and manageable guidelines on how to get through these potential pitfall areas.

So when procrastination looks like it's going to take hold, remember to break your task down into smaller pieces, switch your focus, set yourself time challenges, reward yourself for the efforts made, and make sure that you look after your health. Remember, your health is the most important tool you own. There is no point in compromising your health in your pursuit of wealth, only to then find yourself spending that wealth trying to regain lost health!

Here is a worksheet for you to use to identify the reasons that you know have caused you to procrastinate in important tasks. Alongside each procrastination stumbling block, turn it on its head and think of ways that would work for you to overcome that cause of procrastination and move you forward:

	Cause of procrastination:		Solution to procrastination:
1.		1.	
2.		2.	
3.		3.	
4.		4	

Just get going!

SO now we're well on our way along our goal journey. You're feeling well planned and in control. You're focused on what you're doing now, rather than worrying about what you'll be tackling next month, and you're watching your highlighted and achieved mini-goals mount up and move you closer and closer to your destination. It's looking good, your energy levels are high, and then inexplicably something happens,

And that's what step eight is about:

Step 8

Dealing with your slumps

"Even if you're on the right track, you'll get run over if you just sit there"
- Will Rogers

We often look at successful people around us and think that they're somehow more super-human than we are, because they never seem to suffer from feeling down in the dumps, or just experiencing a general slump. But of course the truth is, they do. We all do. Our brilliant mood and our fizzing energy of one day can be replaced by a feeling of "what's the point" and "I can't be bothered" seemingly overnight.

Who knows why this happens (although if we were to get technical, it can often be explained by variations in the chemical processes and balance in our bodies, but this is not the time nor the place for a discussion on your internal mechanisms!) But how do we cope with these "off" times without letting them have a negative impact on our goal achievement?

Well this is an area that does differ so much from person to person, so for this step, I'll cover a few of the approaches that work well for the majority of my delegates.

Firstly, you probably know better than anyone else, how badly these mini moods or mini depressive periods affect you. You're best equipped to know how long they tend to last, and most importantly, you are probably quite aware of the fact that, as quickly as a slump might have hit, it will just as quickly take its leave.

So be honest with yourself. You know it's going to be temporary. You know you'll emerge out the other end with your normal bounce in your step (and by the time you've seen major progress towards your important goals, you'll be amazed at how much bounce you'll HAVE in your step!), so don't beat yourself up about it.

When a slump is upon you, make sure you're eating well, sleeping efficiently, and perhaps give yourself a day off from your steady progress. If you know that slumps are a common problem for yourself, factor this into your goal achievement timelines, but don't be indulgent about it. The more you pander to your slumps, the more they'll plague you. But recognising that it may just be your mind and body's sign that you need to slow down a little is perfectly okay.

Secondly, often a brilliant way to break out of lethargy, or negativity, or indifference, or whatever form(s) your slumps take, is some exercise. Just getting up, getting outside, and getting your blood flowing and your heart beating a little faster, breathing a little deeper and experiencing movement in your muscles, encouraging circulation of your lymph glands. (Be honest – you didn't expect me to mention lymph glands here! A bit more on this later in this step...) This lifts your moods, cleans your body and clears your mind.

Thirdly, it's often quite motivating to look at all your lovely highlighted, achieved steps, and remind yourself just how much you've already done. Look through those achievements and remind yourself that some of the things you've got done are tasks that you were nervous about, or were outside of your knowledge boundaries, or were actually quite difficult, but still you did them. And probably if you're honest with yourself, you're most proud of the steps you achieved that were the most challenging, and moved us the furthest out of our comfort zones. Sometimes just a reminder of our capability and passion is a great way of snapping out of a slump!

Fourthly, try, even when you're feeling quite switched off, to achieve something positive with your day. I get a kick out of a routine I developed quite early on in my personal journey towards achieving my goals: Every night when I climb into bed and before I go to bed, I write down in a little notebook three things that I've done today that have made it a day worth living.

Sometimes the things I write down are quite big things, and sometimes they seem quite small things, comparatively speaking, but every single one of them has made that day worthwhile. It might be a walk, a big job of work done, and my fridge cleaned out. It might be a long shower during which inspiration struck, a talk with a friend or colleague that got me thinking differently about something, and it might be a rewarding and enjoyable lunch date with some good friends, but I always make sure there are at least three things that I can write in my notebook.

This sounds like an odd thing to say, but if you come on one of my programmes, this will start to make more sense to you. I always wake up in the morning and think "If this is my last day on Earth, what would I want to achieve or do with this day?" I firmly believe that every single day that we wake up to, is a real privilege and gift, and it is a gift that we get given every single morning of our life.

The trouble is, at the end of that day, that gift is gone, and in its place we have the memories and feelings of satisfaction we get from a gift well spent. So that is the price we pay every day for the gift of another 24 hours – using them positively. And every day I want to have at least three legitimate things in my little notebook.

So what I do, just in case, is an hour or so before I go to bed I have a think through what is going to go in my notebook for that day. If I can't think of anything, I have an hour in which I can DO something to add into my little notebook. I'll look for three quick or smaller mini-tasks, and do them. I can be found, at 11pm, sorting out my files, or writing an important document, or cleaning the bathroom, or anything that I've decided is positive progress towards making my life, and the life of those I love, better for my use of my "today".

I call this my "Before bed challenge", so that way even if my day started off a bit slowly because of a slump, I can still turn it around and go to bed with that sense of satisfaction. The good news is that the more positively you start viewing yourself, as you conquer goals that propel you forwards towards your dream future, the less you'll find yourself falling prey to these slumps. You'll find you just don't have the time or inclination to let them happen!

I mentioned lymph glands a bit earlier in this step, so I owe you a short elaboration, although health is a whole different area of my programme, on the role they play in our bodies:

In simple terms, we have two sets of vessels running all around our bodies – one is our blood vessels, and one is our lymphatic pathways. Both of these systems have very important tasks to perform, and one of the numerous tasks they have in common is the cleansing of our bodies. Helping to take the "junk" out of our systems.

Most people are pretty well versed on blood vessels – they deliver oxygen to our cells, take out the carbon dioxide, dump the carbon dioxide into our lungs, pick up a new dose of oxygen, and carry on the process. We know that our blood is pumped around our bodies by an incredibly clever and efficient little muscle, called our heart.

But let's look at our oft-neglected lymphatic system. Equally important, this system effectively collects toxins and waste products from our system and dumps that waste into our waste disposal systems (our kidneys, liver, lungs, etc). Once it's released its rubbish, it trots right back around your body and does the same thing all over again. However, there is a bit of a challenge with your lymph system, and that is that it doesn't have a dedicated muscle pushing it around your body. Instead, it relies on the movement of your muscles, and the expansion and contraction of your lungs, as its main assistors.

Now think about two things we are often guilty of in our current lifestyles – first, we breathe badly, and second, we move little. Think of what that's doing to our beleaguered lymph system! It start moving sluggishly, becomes overloaded with rubbish that isn't being cleaned out of it often enough, and it is therefore not able to pick up our ongoing production of toxins and waste products from our body, leaving our very cells weighed down and heavy with, well, rubbish!

It doesn't take a rocket scientist to figure out the results of this in how we feel. Sluggish, lethargic, achy, fed up, down in the dumps... If any of these sound familiar, do yourself two favours: make a point of breathing properly (and I will quite happily forward you information on this if you'd like – just drop me a line), and make a point of doing some sort of activity every day that uses your muscles, enabling them to massage your lymph system and improve its ability to serve you well!

Just a final word before I finish this step. Oddly, very often the time when a slump will hit hardest is just before our grand finale. When our end goal is clearly in sight. And often it's keeping up that final part of the journey that gives us our biggest challenge, which leads us on to step nine...

Step 9

Maintaining momentum

*"Perseverance is not a long race; it is many short races
one after another".*
Walter Elliot

So how do we keep going, week in and week out. How do we
keep focus, not get distracted, and not get sucked into the

negativity that perhaps surrounds us? What is the best way of really keeping that wheel turning, the energy levels high, the focus intact, and our dreams and goals alive? Well, luckily this is one of the more "positive" problems we're likely to encounter along our goal journey-line, and there are some good, solid pieces of information that I can share with you here that all help either by the knowing or by the doing, in maintaining your positive momentum.

Firstly, let's discuss one of the biggest challenges we might find ourselves facing at different stages in this journey. Challenge one is the fact that we still need to carry on with our real life, and for some goals, this is the case, until we reach that critical tipping point where you can give up what you currently do to keep a roof over your head and food on your table, and move into doing whatever your goal may have been in preparation for the career you want to move into.

This is tricky, because what happens with change-of-career type goals, is that there is often a series of steps that we have to climb from where we are now, to where we want to be. So for example, perhaps you want to move from working for someone else, to having your own business. You've put in all the grunt work, created your business plan, got the systems in place, get your costings sorted, etc. (These of course will be steps along the journey-line to this specific goal, and if you need more knowledge or guidance on creating a new business from scratch, please contact my office and speak to us about that particular course that we run.)

Perhaps you've started your new profession in a small way, providing your services or products for a few clients along the way, but you still aren't in a position to give up your full time job. The fact is that, when we're doing really worth while goals like moving into a career area that you feel really passionate about, you will always have a perhaps particularly stressful period where you are, literally juggling a bit more than you can manage long term.

When this happens, we need to keep focus on our new career goals, and know that the hard work will pay off in spades. Try and be creative in thinking through methods in which you could ease this pressure. For example, perhaps you can reduce your hours at the job you're looking at leaving. Or perhaps you can rope in the help of a family member or friend for a couple of months to help get your new business off the ground, and keep the momentum going.

You might find that you can take leave owed to you, or employ someone to perhaps do some of the work in other areas of your life. For example, if 10 hours of your time will secure you £1000 of income, you're effectively being paid £100 per each of those hours.

If you pay someone £10 per hour to do your cleaning or gardening, or filing, you could redistribute these saved hours into the business, and effectively end up £90 better off for each of those hours, and you could have another satisfied client in the growth of your new fledgling business.

Have an exit plan clear in your head. Perhapsyou've decided that when you've got enough money in your account to fund your next 6 months, that's when you're going to hand in your notice. You decide what point is comfortable for you, but at some stage you are going to have to take the leap, and have the faith that your hard work is going to pay off.

We often, strangely, fear the ultimate achievement of our goals, and there are usually two reasons for this. One, if we reach our goal, where do we put all the time and energy we so enjoy spending in achieving something fabulous? Where do you go from your now completed goal? And two, what happens if that goal doesn't bring us the level of happiness and satisfaction we were hoping for?

Well, the truth is that you will never run out of goals to pursue, things to achieve, adventures to enjoy and places to explore, Once you develop the wonderful habit of goal achievement, you'll always be looking at what you can do next. It is addictive, but in the most positive of ways: Feeling the rush of excitement and pride that comes from well invested time and energy is priceless. Seeing dreams become your reality is so empowering, you'll find yourself feeling excited about the next goal, and the next, and the next. As long as you're alive and breathing, you'll find you have goals that you would love to achieve. You have set the framework for such a great life, and you'll deserve to reap every reward that comes your way.

And secondly, no goal is ever really complete. Chances are that when you reach what you thought was your big goal, there is another level of that goal that you want to achieve. This is perfectly healthy and positive. If you've written one successful book, chances are you'll set yourself a goal of writing a second great book. Running a good local business may inspire you to expand across your county, your country, and possibly even internationally in time.

What you'll also discover is that, as the momentum is created and maintained, it becomes easier to do the parts of the journey that are less appealing, because the ultimate picture will becoming clearer and clearer in your mind. And when each piece of the process is seen to move you forward, it becomes much more satisfying to do!

I love vision boards as a method of keeping focus and maintaining momentum. Look for pictures that illustrate your goals, slogans, sayings or mottos that inspire you. Quotes that stir your blood, and put them all together on a vision board. It does work on your computer, if you don't feel inclined to do a physical board, but then use it as your screen saver, or make sure that you look at it several times a day. Having it tucked away in a folder on your computer pretty much defeats its purpose!

Just a word of warning. Unfortunately some of your friends will be a lot less supportive of your progress than you would like. Some of them may belittle it, and unfortunately, some of them will actually try to stop your progress, and pull you back to your starting point. Why does this happen, and how can you cope with it?

Your friends may well be perfectly happy with the relationship that they have with their current version of you. And perhaps they fear if you're slimmer/wealthier/more educated, you won't be the same lovely person you are right now, and they might wonder if they'll get on with that new version of you. Also, they might fear that you'll reject them, or look down on them, or outgrow them.

The other problem is that, by actually putting in the effort and making such great changes for the better in your life, you're reminding them of their own inadequacies, or lack of focus, or un-achieved dreams. What you'll find is that they will probably react in one of three ways: firstly, they'll watch your progress and applaud your successes, secondly, they may be inspired by your achievements, and join you by making really good positive progress towards their own goals, or thirdly, that green eyed, jealous monster who probably now feels rather lazy and inadequate, will try and bring you down, and try and stop your progress or belittle your every move.

You need to be strong enough to stand up for what you want. You need to know that anybody who needs you to remain unfulfilled and mediocre in order to be your friend, is probably not someone that you're going to naturally move forward into your future with anyway.

They say that a man can often be judged by the quality of the people that he can call his friends, and often this is true. There are so many people in the world who revel in hardship, love gossiping about everyone in a normally completely un-positive way, and love comparing notes on how lousy their lives are, that it fascinates me! If the highlight of your day is bitching in the supermarket queue, or complaining about life when you're gathered at the school gates, then how can you possibly be surprised by your life not being as positive and profitable as the life of others! You get what you focus on. Focus on the negative, and your life may well get stuck in a really lousy place along the journey, Focus on the positive, and your life journey will be far more rewarding and satisfying!

Decide who YOU are, and what YOU aspire to, and have the guts to stick to your guns! Those who come with you into your future are probably the types of friendships you value the most. Don't let the laziness or lack of motivation of those around you, hold YOU back from YOUR destiny!

A great help to most people is to have a professional Mentor who will keep them focused, help them to overcome challenges, and when necessary, give them a kick up the backside. A good Mentor is a great find. They will be as passionate as you are about your goals and dreams. They will know how to help you tackle obstacles or roadblocks that may emerge along the way.

They will have extensive knowledge, and most importantly, will have walked the walk themselves.

Be wary of life coaches who have limited training, and limited life experience, They will often be more focused on their journey than on yours. Pick someone that you "Click" with. That is approachable and easy to work with, has high energy levels and a constructive and practical approach to dealing with the challenges you may encounter. And very importantly, make sure it is someone you can trust completely, because they will ideally be your brainstorming partner, your advisor, your confidante, and the person who will celebrate your successes right alongside you! They will, if chosen carefully, be the biggest asset you have in your journey towards greatness!

And now on to the final step in our incredible journey....

Step 10

Celebrating your successes!

"The more you praise and celebrate in life, the more there is to praise and celebrate!"
Oprah Winfrey

No matter how big your goals become, never, ever let it overshadow the goals that you have achieved. If you hadn't achieved goal number one, goals two, three and four would never have been possible. Always take the time to celebrate your successes, and give yourself permission to feel really good about yourself.

This is not a time for humility or self-effacing behaviour. This is you feeling on top of the world, proud of your successes, amazed at your ability to achieve what may have once seemed completely impossible, and having a celebration.

Try to reward yourself with something that is really meaningful to you. A lovely dinner out in your beautiful dress that you can now slip into easily might be the perfect reward for your weight loss goals. A trip to the country of the language you've studied might be a dream come true. A lovely new car when you reach a financial target might be just the incentive you need to push forward.

But there are "smaller" rewards that can be used for the sub-goals along the way. A lovely back massage, or a trip to a local attraction you've never been to could be a great reward. A long hot bubble bath might be an indulgence that you could look forward to on the weekend, following successful completion of that week's mini-goals. Lunch with a good friend, or a good bottle of wine might warm the cockles of your heart. The list is endless!

For rewards to work most effectively, make them something different to things that you do for yourself anyway. The more special or different they are, the more power they will have to incentivise you. If you take yourself off for monthly manicures anyway, it won't motivate you to have a manicure as a goal reward as it will be an also-ran type of reward. However, if you love a pedicure but feel it's a bit too much of an indulgence on a regular basis, that could be added to your manicure and give you a feeling of extra indulgence and reward.

And very importantly, discipline yourself. DO NOT take the reward unless you've earned it! If you do that, you're completely defeating the purpose of your reward! So hold off on booking that Italian trip until you've finished the Italian course. Hold the reward until you can really revel in it and know, with every fibre of your being, that that reward is rightfully yours, hard won, and a celebration of an amazing accomplishment!

Final word

Congratulations for having the motivation and determination to invest in yourself and in the achievement of your potential! We are all capable of achieving so many fantastic things, but the fact is that not many people have got the "spark" that is needed to actually get on with creating their destiny. The majority of people will muddle along, as best they can, and never have the courage to push themselves out of their comfort zone. You have already singled yourself out from that crowd, and I look forward to learning some of what you have achieved!

This book is part of a series of a much greater whole, so if you found it useful to you, please contact us and let's see what else we have available that will help you to Live a Life you Love. Our resources include books, webinars, reports, online workshops and support tools. And of course additionally, we do many in-depth live programmes and workshops, for which we get excellent reviews. We would love to meet you and share your journey with you.

I can be contacted via my website: www.newlevels.co.uk, or by email: info@newlevels.co.uk. We would love to hear your success stories!

My wish for you is that you continue to grow and learn, and stretch your horizons so wide, that your life exceeds your wildest dreams!

Thank you, and may your God bless you.

Jane

Learn to Live
a Life you Love

Now read about our flagship programme...

180/180

Turn <u>Your</u> Life Through 180 degrees in 180 days

Helping you create the true wealth that comes from whole-life balance; not just a "workshop" or "intensive", but a SIX MONTH programme to guide you on <u>your</u> journey of change.

A <u>6 month hands-on mentoring programme</u> designed to help <u>you</u>

- think outside your current box
- create goals & timelines
- achieve better work/life balance

With our ongoing support over a full 180 days, you will learn

- how to practically recognise and overcome the fears and insecurities that are holding you back
- the six things you must know to break out of your holding pattern
- how to create a template for maximising your whole-life potential
- how to harness the psychology of progress, not procrastination
- how to goal set properly, creating a realistic and manageable template for change.

180/180

Programme Highlights

- Three full-day live workshops (Sat or Sun)

- Full-day kick-off event – **"Achievement Accelerator"**

- **"Progress Step-Up Bootcamp"** (day 60 approx)

- **"Success Stars Seminar"** (day 180 approx)

- Ten two-hour webinars

- Six hours of 1-2-1 coaching sessions with Jane

- Awards ceremony & dinner

- Your personal "Journey Of Change" journal, compiled throughout the 180 days

Psychology of Wealth Two-Day Workshop

Learn how to stop your sub-conscious from costing you money!

Key areas covered in this fascinating two-day interactive workshop include:

> Recognising the key elements why our relationship with money is flawed.

> How our subconscious mind messes with our ability to make, or keep, money

> Why we fear failure, and why our fear of success is even greater than our fear of failure

> What differentiates the haves from the have-nots

> Why some goals seem particularly difficult to achieve, while others seem relatively easily

> The subconscious way we repel the very money we want to attract

> Why those who win lotteries or make easy money, tend to lose it all quickly

- Why "enough" is a goal post that keeps moving!

- Healthy money management vs unhealthy money usage

- Why we are raising a generation who have a flawed understanding of money

- Are we damaging our children's ability to create personal success?

- Why more businesses go bust then go bang

- Does saving money work?

- Why money doesn't buy happiness

"New Levels" for business

A qualified doctor of psychology, with additional business degrees in both marketing and communication, as well as several other post-graduate qualifications, Jane brings a unique blend of cutting-edge theoretical knowledge and real-world pragmatic expertise to her business consulting.

Her in-depth knowledge of business success strategies, international expertise, cutting edge intervention techniques, and her psychological insight into what makes both people and their businesses tick, give her a unique perspective on how to keep a business afloat, accelerate its growth, and differentiate it from its competitors. If you're looking for a fresh, dynamic and motivating approach to breathing life back into business, Jane is the resource you have been looking for.

While Jane has experience in almost all areas of management & leadership development her focus is on:

- actualising leadership potential in their senior executives
- creating high-performing teams
- creating more effective, engaging, creative and sustainable cultures.
- strategic intervention and assistance

She has worked with major global corporations (see below) as well as many small to mid-sized businesses, with senior business leaders, "high potentials", and entrepreneurs.

Jane has a strong track record of working with leaders to develop leadership presence, transform difficult relationships, enhance effective communication and influencing skills and build confidence.

Specific assignments typically include but are not limited to:

- Intensive one-on-one executive training and coaching
- Multi-level corporate coaching; speech-writing and presentation technique
- Direction and training for top-level executives in listed companies and large multi-nationals
- Mentoring and training during corporate restructuring and staff re-organisation
- Confidential short- and long-term goal setting and general guidance in both business and personal arenas across middle and top management
- Training on conflict management
- Training on (and often assisting with execution of) internal & external crisis management:
- Negotiation skills and techniques (and interventions if required)
- Full day intensive workshops across management, leadership, relationship and sales arenas, and psychological insights into the above
- Inter-cultural training, business relationship and management techniques

- ➤ Business breakthrough workshops, to stimulate and create change and growth

Her global client base includes -

PepsiCo
Toyota
Nokia
Telkom SA
Roche Pharmaceuticals
Alfa Romeo
UK Border Agency
Nandos
Plascon Paints
United Nations

Project examples

Every business has its own particular challenges and characteristics. While we have tried and tested intervention tools, we will never allow your business to be treated in a "one size fits all" fashion. We will <u>always</u> treat your business according to it's own personality, and anything that needs to be bespoke to your business will be tailored to fit your needs, rather than you being adjusted for our convenience!

That said some of the "off the shelf" interventions and workshops we *would* recommend include:

Communication Quadrant: *Excellent communication is multi-faceted; are you really giving the message you think you are? Let Jane raise your "CQ" to new levels.*

Enterprise Therapy: *This unique application of psychotherapeutic techniques applied to the workplace will surface and address deep-seated, and often unsuspected, barriers to growth & progress.*

Human Map: *Using a range of bespoke diagnostic tools, developed and validated across international multi-sector clients, Human Map enables a business to attain complete alignment & commitment to mission, vision, values & goals.*

Breakout Bootcamp*: Thought-provoking, energising, and exciting, a Breakout Bootcamp will take you out of your comfort zone and open your mind to your potential as never before*

Business Client Testimonials

Read what Jane's corporate clients have to say:

"Your ability to cut through to the nub of the issue never fails to impress me. In forty years in business I have never met anyone as insightful as you."
John Halker, MD Guernsey Flowers Ltd

"When I joined the JD Group I had no idea how much the new Personal Services Division would be part of my life. It all started with you and you should look back with great pride on what it's become. Thanks for your strength and for keeping us in line and on track, and for never letting us compromise on our objectives."
Mark Richards, Finance & Special Projects Director, JD Group

"Thanks to you too for being so great at what you do – you guys are rockstars!"
Greg Secker, Chairman & CEO Knowledge to Action Ltd

"An extensive background in senior management, coupled with strong creative flair, leads to some great ideas! Unlike many consultants or advisors I have encountered these guys have an innate understanding of the financial & operational aspects of doing business and they are always realistic, practical and pragmatic."

Gary Grose, Regional Agency Officer Southeast Asia, Allstate International

"You did a great job with our new field salesforce – we would not hesitate to use your services again."
Clive Fielder, Marketing Director, Premier Foods / PepsiCo Southern Africa

"I really enjoyed working with you; you are hard-working, reliable, and diligent but with a great sense of humour and the ability to keep problems in perspective. I would not hesitate to recommend you."
Mark Casey, General Manager, Festo International

"I have been very happy with the results of the project we have worked on together, and been highly impressed with your obvious extensive knowledge of sales & marketing, particularly as it applies to international markets. One point that is worthy of specific comment is their realistic & financially prudent approach – ideas are always supported by clear and logical financial arguments, a rare and welcome change to my past experience with consultants. I would not hesitate to recommend their services."
Phil Rowcliffe, President Director, Axa Insurance (Indonesia)

Feedback from Jane's Recent Events

4. Do you have any feedback for your presenter?

Jane was absolutely excellent, I would be very interested if she was to do a longer course at KZA.

2. Do you have any additional feedback on the service provided prior to t

Jane is lovely inspirational clearly dedicated to her work

2. Do you have any additional feedback on the service provided pri

JANE WAS FANTASTIC

Check out her website for upcoming events
near you
www.newlevels.co.uk

"You only need to achieve the "impossible" once, for all things to become possible."

Dr Jane Cox

Made in the USA
San Bernardino, CA
12 December 2016